W9-BEU-148

Lisa Owings

Lerner Publications ◆ Minneapolis

On the cover: Team Secret wins their fourth ESL One championship in Birmingham, England, in 2019.

Lerner Publications Company
An imprint of Lerner Publishing Group, Inc.
241 First Avenue North
Minneapolis, MN 55401 USA

For reading levels and more information, look up this title at www.lernerbooks.com.

Main body text set in ITC Franklin Gothic Std.
Typeface provided by Adobe Systems.

Editor: Alison Lorenz **Designer:** Viet Chu

Library of Congress Cataloging-in-Publication Data

Names: Owings, Lisa, author. | Lerner Publishing Group, Inc.
Title: Gaming's greatest moments / Lisa Owings.
Description: Minneapolis : Lerner Publications, 2021. | Series: The Best of Gaming (UpDog Books) | Includes bibliographical references and index. | Audience: Ages 8–13 years | Audience: Grades K–1 | Summary: "Whether it's a new high score, a devastating attack, or an incredible come-from-behind win, pro gaming is full of amazing moments. Learn about the athletes, teams, and moments that thrill fans around the world"— Provided by publisher.
Identifiers: LCCN 2019049906 (print) | LCCN 2019049907 (ebook) | ISBN 9781541590519 (Library Binding) | ISBN 9781728414089 (Paperback) | ISBN 9781728401171 (eBook)
Subjects: LCSH: Video games—History. | Video games—Competition—Juvenile literature. | Video games—Social aspects—Juvenile literature. | Video games industry—Juvenile literature. | Video gamers—Juvenile literature. | Computer games—Social aspects—Juvenile literature. | Internet games. | Competition (Psychology)
Classification: LCC GV1469.3 .0947 2020 (print) | LCC GV1469.3 (ebook) |DDC 794.8—dc23

LC record available at https://lccn.loc.gov/2019049906
LC ebook record available at https://lccn.loc.gov/2019049907

Manufactured in the United States of America
1-47570-48100-2/11/2020

Table of Contents

The $6 Million Echo Slam

The Evil Geniuses (EG) needed one more victory. Then they would win The International 2015, the world's biggest *Dota 2* contest.

They were up against the Chinese Dota Elite Community (CDEC), who were playing well. But CDEC had all their heroes in one spot.

heroes: characters used in play

EG's Ice Blast let them see their targets. Then Earthshaker blinked in for the Echo Slam.

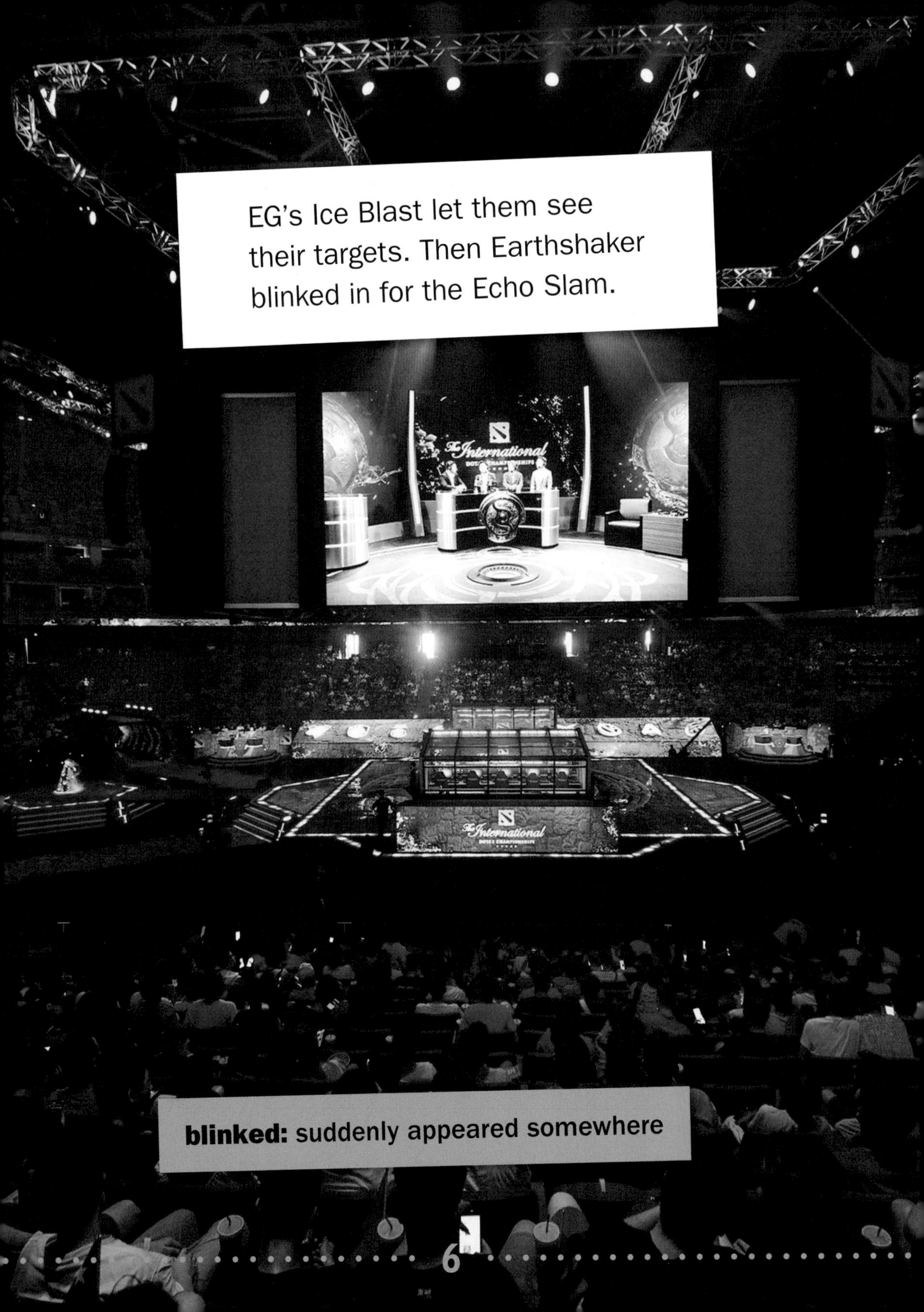

blinked: suddenly appeared somewhere

It wiped out all but one CDEC player.
The attack won EG $6 million.

Esports is full of exciting moments!

esports: video games played in contests

Gamer Tips: *Dota 2*

- Talk to your team. Work together.
- Find runes in the river. They power up your hero.
- Beat Roshan. Get a special item.
- Use in-game guides.

UP NEXT!

ANOTHER GREAT MOMENT IN GAMING HISTORY.

Evo Moment 37

Evo 2004 ended with a huge comeback.

Evo: stands for Evolution Championship Series, a series of fighting game contests

comeback: a win after falling behind

Street Fighter player Daigo Umehara had just one health point. Justin Wong went in for the win.

BIO BREAK!

Name: Daigo Umehara
Age: 38
Hometown: Tokyo, Japan
Claim to fame: best *Street Fighter* comeback

Name: Elijah "4DRStorm"
Age: 16
Home country: United States
Claim to fame: won match in Ninja Vegas '18

Name: Marielle "Layla" Louise
Home country: Canada
Claim to fame: first female *Dota 2* player to make a major qualifier

qualifier: an early match whose winners go on to compete in the finals

Name: Saahil "UNiVeRsE" Arora
Age: 30
Hometown: Madison, Wisconsin
Claim to fame: used Echo Slam to win The International in 2015

Name: Ricki "HelloKittyRicki" Ortiz
Age: 36
Hometown: San Francisco Bay Area, California
Claim to fame: top *Street Fighter* player

Name: Tyler "Ninja" Blevins
Age: 28
Hometown: Grayslake, Illinois
Claim to fame: most popular streamer

streamer: a gamer who posts live videos online

Umehara chose to parry. He needed perfect timing.

parry: to counter an attack

Umehara parried an amazing fifteen attacks in a row. He came back from near defeat to win the game.

Ninja Vegas '18

In 2018, Tyler "Ninja" Blevins invited pros and fans to play with him in Las Vegas.

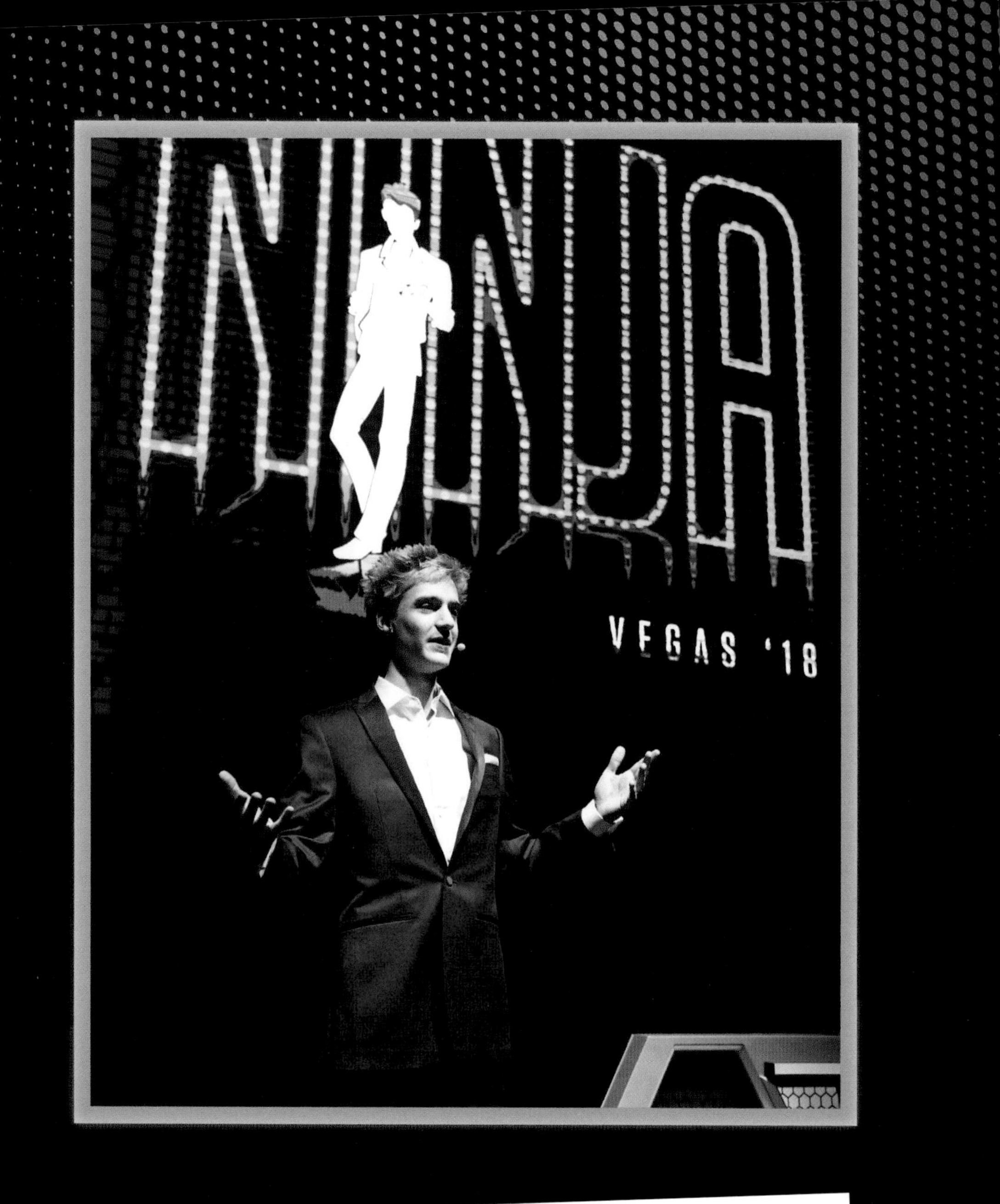

Anyone who beat him won $2,500 per game. When Ninja won, he gave the money to Alzheimer's research.

Fans loved the chance to meet Ninja and show off their skills.

Vegas '18 was Ninja's most viewed stream ever.

stream: a live video posted online

Gaming is full of great moments. Millions watch esports events.

It’s amazing to catch that epic win live!

Glossary

blinked: suddenly appeared somewhere

comeback: a win after falling behind

esports: video games played in contests

Evo: stands for Evolution Championship Series, a series of fighting game contests

heroes: characters used in play

parry: to counter an attack

qualifier: an early match whose winners go on to compete in the finals

stream: a live video posted online

streamer: a gamer who posts live videos online

Check It Out!

Dota 2: The International
http://www.dota2.com/international/overview/
Read all about the biggest tournament in esports.

Guinness World Records. *Guinness World Records: Gamer's Edition 2020.* London: Guinness World Records, 2019.
Meet the world record holders of gaming.

Online Gaming Tips for Kids, Teens and Tweens
https://staysafeonline.org/resource/stop-think-connect-online-gaming-tips-kids-teens-tweens/
Stay safe while gaming with these tips.

Owings, Lisa. *The World of Esports.* Minneapolis: Lerner Publications, 2021.
Dive into the world of competitive esports.

Pettman, Kevin. *Esports Superstars.* London: Carlton Books, 2018.
Check out the biggest names and events in esports.

Scratch
https://scratch.mit.edu/
Try making your own videos and games.

Index

Photo Acknowledgments

Image credits: Suzi Pratt/FilmMagic/Getty Images, p. 4; Hu Chengwei/Getty Images, pp. 5, 6, 8; Courtesy of Evil Geniuses, pp. 7, 13; Joe Buglewicz/Getty Images, pp. 10, 15; Leonel Calara/Shutterstock.com, p. 11; Daniel Shirey/Getty Images, p. 14; Ethan Miller/Getty Images, pp. 16, 17, 19; Brace Hemmelgarn/Minnesota Twins/Getty Images, p. 18; Johannes Eisele/AFP/Getty Images, p. 20; Rebeca Figueiredo Amorim/Getty Images, p. 21.

Cover: Luke Walker/Getty Images; cundra/Getty Images.